Niles Public Library District
6960 Oakton Street • Niles, Illinois 60714
Phone 847-663-1234

DATE DUE	DATE DUE

North American Indian Games

Madelyn Klein Anderson

Franklin Watts
A Division of Grolier Publishing
New York • London • Hong Kong • Sydney
Danbury, Connecticut

Note to readers: Definitions for words in **bold** can be found in the Glossary at the back of this book.

Photographs ©: Art Resource, NY: 7, 20, 21 (National Museum of American Art, Washington DC.); Corbis-Bettmann: 52 (UPI), 28; Courtesy Museum of New Mexico: 30, 31; Dennis Sanders: 43 (Clinton Stewart); John Running: 53; Liaison Agency, Inc.: 48 (L. Novovitch), 12 (Rotolo); Malcolm Brenner: 38, Peter Arnold Inc.: 4 (Martha Cooper); Photo Researchers: 50 (Jim Zipp); Reinhard Brucker: 3, 10, 16, 17, 19, 22, 24 bottom, 32, 33, 35, 42; Sun Valley Video & Photography: 9, 24 top, 34, 44, 45 (Marilyn "Angel" Wynn); Superstock, Inc.: 26, 27, 40; Tony Stone Images: 11 (Amwell); Underwood Photo Archives: 8; Yosemite Museum Collection: 14, 15.

Cover illustration by Gary Overacre; Joan M. Toro: 47.

Visit Franklin Watts on the Internet at:
http://publishing.grolier.com

Library of Congress Cataloging-in-Publication Data

Anderson, Madelyn Klein.
    North American Indian games / Madelyn Klein Anderson.
        p.   cm.— (Watts Library)
    Includes bibliographical references and index.
    Summary: Examines the origins, nature, and significance of games played by North American Indians, including shinny and other ball games, dice games, and guessing games.
    ISBN: 0-531-20403-0 (lib. bdg.)   0-531-16474-8 (pbk.)
    1. Indians of North America—Games Juvenile literature. 2. Indians of North America—Rites and ceremonies Juvenile literature. [1. Indians of North America—Games. 2. Games] I. Title. II. Series.
E98.G2A53   2000
394`.3—dc21
                                99-30240
                                   CIP

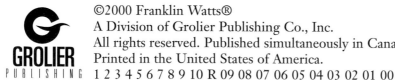

©2000 Franklin Watts®
A Division of Grolier Publishing Co., Inc.
All rights reserved. Published simultaneously in Canada.
Printed in the United States of America.
1 2 3 4 5 6 7 8 9 10 R 09 08 07 06 05 04 03 02 01 00

Contents

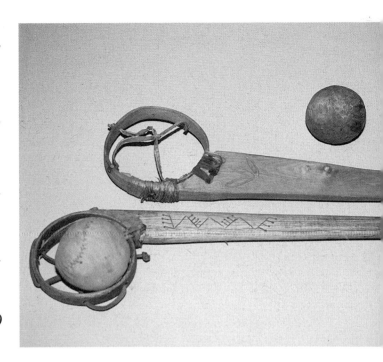

An Apache coming of age ceremony

Chapter One

The Fabric of Tribal Life

Games were part of everyday life in all North American Indian tribes. Indians played games for pleasure and for traditional celebrations and religious ceremonies, such as births and deaths. The Micmacs of eastern Canada, for example, celebrated weddings with a day of dancing, a day of foot ball, a day of a game called shinny, and a final day of dice. Indians looked to games for signs of what the future would bring. They also held games to heal the sick and to train for war.

A Cherokee Legend

Games are part of many tribal stories handed down from generation to generation, such as this one from the Cherokees:

The animals once challenged the birds to a ball game. The great hawk and the eagle took their position in the trees, along with the other birds. On the ground were the bear, whose heavy weight could smother the opposition, the deer, who was the best of runners, and the **terrapin,** *whose shell kept it from feeling the hardest of blows. Just before the game began, the birds saw two tiny animals, like mice, climbing the tree on which the captain of the birds sat. The little animals asked to be allowed to play with the birds. The captain pointed to their four feet and said, "You are animals. Why do you want to play with us?" The little animals replied that they had been turned away by the other animals, who had laughed at them because they were so small. The birds felt badly and wanted the two little ones to play, but how could they if they had no wings? They looked around and spotted the dance drum with its head of groundhog skin. Quickly they cut a small piece of skin from it and shaped it into a pair of wings. They attached the wings to one of the little animals, and thus the bat, Tlameha, was born. But what of the other little animal? All the groundhog skin was used up. The eagle and the hawk came to the rescue with their strong beaks. Each took one side of the little animal in its beak and pulled and stretched its skin into wings. And so Tewa, the flying squirrel, was made. Then Tlameha and Tewa flew the ball over, under, and around all the animals on the ground and won the game for the birds.*

Cherokee men sometimes put bits of flying squirrel or bat skins on their playing sticks. They believed this would give them the swiftness and **agility** of these animals. To move like birds, the Choctaws wore a large **plume** suspended from their belts. The ball players of most tribes often wore little or no clothing. Instead of clothing, the men usually decorated themselves with paints in bold, bright patterns.

Ball players wore feathers, hoping to imitate the speed and keen sight of birds.

7

Small gourds and some string make good playthings for these children.

A Variety of Games

Indian nations throughout North America played many different games. They also played their own versions of similar games.

Everyone Could Play

Indian games were not played by specially trained athletes. Nor was a team made up of a specific number of players. All who wanted to could play. There were few rules, and players did not have to be athletic, although a good player was appreciated. While most tribes had separate games for men and women, others allowed both genders to play. Children played their own games or imitated adult games using safer equipment. Equipment varied in size and type. Balls might be round or baggy, made of **buckskin,** blanket material, or rock. A playing field could be 25 miles (40 kilometers) long or the size of a school playground, depending on the land and the number of players. Goalposts could be natural boundaries, such as trees or a rock, or poles set in the ground, or even two blankets set side by side.

Gambling

Most Indians gambled heavily on the outcome of games played for pleasure. (Indians did not gamble on games played for religious purposes.) Even children's games might have small bets, such as a slingshot or pebble, to make the game more challenging. Horses, clothes, blankets, weapons, jewelry, cooking pots—everything was accepted as a bet.

Shells used for placing bets

Learning About Indian Games

Early explorers, fur trappers, and missionaries who made contact with various tribes described their games in detail in letters, reports, and drawings. The young United States government soon understood the need to find out all it could about the Indians before their culture changed through contact with settlers. Through the newly formed Smithsonian Institution, the government sent **anthropologists** and **ethnologists** to collect oral histories from the storytellers among the tribes. They collected information about legends, music, religious beliefs, and games, which were published in reports to the U.S. Congress. It is from these reports that our information about early Indian games comes.

The Smithsonian Institution

The Smithsonian Institution, located in Washington, D.C., was founded in 1846. Today, it consists of several museums, including the Natural History Museum, the National Air and Space Museum, and the National Museum of American History.

Same Game, Many Names

In the reports to Congress, games were usually given English names because referring to them by their Indian names was impossible. The name for the same game might be different in hundreds of different Indian languages. For example, the Arapaho played "gugahawat," the Cheyenne "ohonistuts," and the Navajos "tsol," but they were all the same game. Since that game resembled an English game called "shinny," it made sense to use the word "shinny." This also kept the reports from favoring one Indian language over others, which might also give the impression that the game was played exclusively by one tribe.

Present-Day Versions

Many North American Indian games may seem familiar to us today. Some people believed that the Europeans brought them to the Indians. But the research done by the Smithsonian ethnologists shows that although many cultures play similar games, the games were developed by the people playing them.

For example, the game known as "badminton" in England and the United States is known as "battledore and shuttlecock" in Japan. Its origin may have been in India or China. The Indians of North America also played it long before contact with other groups. Their **shuttlecocks** were corn cobs or husks stuck with feathers, and the rackets were netted hoops on a handle.

The Navajos claim they invented baseball, but it is believed they learned the game while most of the tribe was imprisoned at Fort Sumner, New Mexico, from 1863 to 1867. However, it is well documented that the Indians did give the rest of the world the game of lacrosse.

Lacrosse is a popular game at many schools today.

Dancers added to the excitement of the games.

Chapter Two

Play Ball!

Sometimes, thousands of Indians would gather for important ball games. The air crackled with the whinnies of horses, the shouts of excited bettors demanding the attention of the old men arranging bets, and the many different songs sung by hundreds of voices accompanied by drums. It was important to make as much noise as possible to attract the attention of the spirits and to distract players on the opposing team into making mistakes.

Rules of Play

The most basic rule in major North American Indian ball games was that the ball was never touched by hand. Use of the hands constituted a foul for the inning or round. Only a few tribes made exceptions to the no-hands rule for games such as foot ball, hand-and-foot ball, and ball tossing and juggling.

Among other rules, some tribes did not allow players to eat rabbit before a game, for fear of taking on the weakness of the rabbit. Nor could a player sit or lie on the ground, which might sap his strength. To rest, he had to lean against someone's back.

Shinny

A stranger challenged the gambling god of the Navajos to a game of tsol (shinny) for the freedom of those who were slaves. The players assembled at the goal line. On one side were the slaves, on the other were the free men. The free men would become slaves of the gambling god if they lost the game, but if they won, the slaves would go free. A little bird spoke to the stranger and offered to carry the ball in her bill if the stranger struck it gently. The first to play was the god, who struck the ball a mighty blow. But the ball did not reach the line. Then the

Two Bats

While most tribes used one bat, the Makahs were the only group known to use two bats.

14

Boys play a rousing game of shinny in the Yosemite Valley.

stranger struck the ball lightly, and the little bird grasped it and flew with it over the line. All the slaves were freed and jumped across the line to greet their relatives with joy.

Shinny is referred to in many Indian legends, not only those of the Navajos. The shinny stick or bat may have represented the club of the War Gods, and the game was sometimes played to honor a god. The Cherokees called the game "little brother of war" because they considered it good training for battle. The Makahs of southwestern Canada played it to celebrate the capture of a whale, which was an important source of food during the winter.

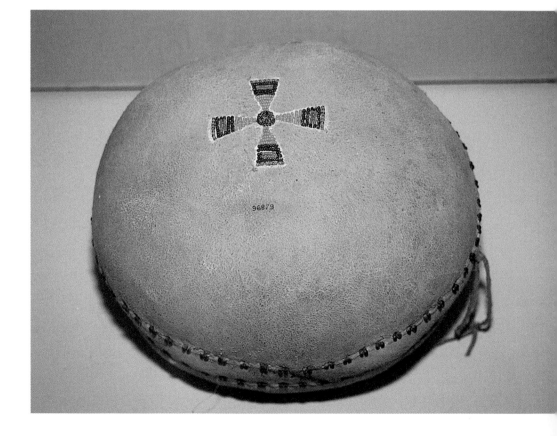

A Cheyenne ball (right), made of sewn animal hide, and a painted Inuit ball (opposite page)

Shinny was played by virtually all tribes. Women often played, sometimes with or against men. A single bat was used to drive a ball across a goal. The bats were slender, with a curved and slightly wide striking end. Shinny players would use their feet to **propel** the ball, but never their hands.

Among the people of the Pacific coast and the Southwest, the ball was usually a knot from a tree trunk. The Navajos used a bag-shaped ball. Eastern and Plains people used a ball of buffalo hair covered with buckskin and painted in different colors. The Makahs used whalebone, and the Inuits of Alaska used a small ivory or bone ball.

Although the distance between goals often was not measured, it was known to range from 200 to 1,400 yards (180 to 1,280 meters) depending on the amount of land that was available and the number of players. The Hopis played shinny on a field with one village as the starting line and another village—sometimes as much as 8 miles (13 km) away—as the goal.

Teams were usually made up of an even number of players. In large games, there could be as many as five hundred players on a team.

Racket

This is the game that became known to French fur trappers, who were the first to make contact with many Indian tribes when much of North America belonged to France. The Frenchmen renamed racket "la cross." A playing field they named "Prairie de la Cross" became popular as a trading post and later as a town and city: La Crosse, Wisconsin.

Many years ago, before there was a moon in the sky, the Cherokees invited their neighbors to a game of baglitaway [racket]. The ball could be handled only with the rackets each man held in either hand. One team handled the rackets so well and ran so well with them that they would surely win. This bothered one of the losing players, and he picked up the ball with his hands and threw it toward the goalposts. The ball rose into the air—but never came down. It stuck in the solid sky, and became the moon. Ever afterward, when the moon became pale and only parts could be seen, the

Racket Fields

The length of the racket field varied. A Mohawk Indian field was usually about 150 yards (137 meters) long. However, the midwestern Miami Indians used a field that was 1.5 miles (2.4 km) long!

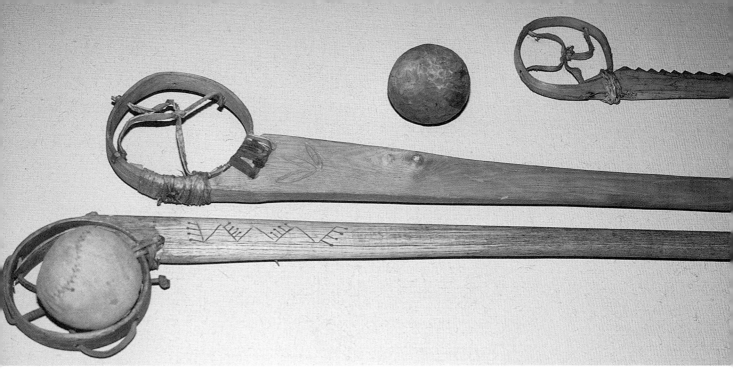

Lacrosse sticks and balls

Cherokees knew that someone was cheating, and they would only play ball when the moon was full.

One or two rackets, long handles with a netted pouch at one end, were held almost horizontally across the body to move the ball through the opposing team to a goalpost. A single goal might win a game or the winner might be the team with the most goals by sundown.

Ten people, or one thousand, could play racket. It was usually a man's game, although women sometimes played it

Important Equipment

Much care went into carving or burning a design into the handle of the racket, which was also decorated with feathers and paint. It took time and skill to make the net on the end of the handle strong enough so that it would carry the ball without tearing.

among themselves. Excellent racket players became as famous as great hunters and warriors. Racket required strength and courage. A good whack with a racket could break an opponent's arm or leg. A player could not complain of injuries, however, without risking being called a coward and shamed in front of the tribe.

Doubleball

This was commonly a women's ball game, although in northern California it was played by men. Some reports told of doubleball games among unmarried women as a way of showing off to potential mates. However, Indian legends feature the game in stories of women escaping from evil men:

Bright-Shining Woman [the Moon] gave the game to women so they could enjoy themselves. A Wichita woman who was fleeing the

In a game of doubleball, women dominate the playing field.

*Doubleball equipment,
from the Pima tribe*

attentions of seven wicked brothers used the doubleball to escape them. When she tossed the doubleball, she hung on to the **thong** *and flew up into the air and over the heads of the men, to escape them forever.*

The idea of the game was to use one or two sticks to carry two connected balls or other objects through a goal. Balancing and snatching was quite a feat, and smashing an opponent was all part of the game. One goal might be all that was needed to win, particularly if the playing field was a half-mile (0.8 km) long, which was not uncommon.

Sticks were slender and had a slight curve at the end to carry the connecting thong of the balls, which were made of wicker, buckskin, or deerskin. Balls and sticks were painted the teams' colors and sometimes decorated with fringe, beads, or paint. Midwestern tribes such as the Sauk and Fox used two small, sand-filled buckskin pads connected by a thong. The Paiute used one larger pad but narrowed it in the middle to eliminate the need for a thong.

Cliff-dwelling Indians of the Southwest also shaped a single game piece into two sections by carving a horseshoe-shaped piece of wood that was narrow at the top for carrying. Later Indian tribes also used pieces of wood in various shapes. These are more properly described as billets rather than balls, despite the name of the game.

Ball Race

This ancient game was played among the Indians of California, the Southwest, and Mexico. The Bannocks of Idaho were the only others known to play ball race.

Over the centuries, superstitions built around the game. Some Hopis refused to allow it to be played, claiming it would bring storms and great winds. The Navajos adopted the game from the Hopis. Ball race was especially popular among the Zunis. All males from the age of eight enjoyed the game from early spring to late fall.

Balls were made of stone or wood, and often were covered with the gum from creosote bushes. Sometimes the ball was really a stick or a ring. Those Hopis who did play ball race used cubes of hair fashioned into a block with the gum of the

A polished stone ball (top), and a Sioux beaded ball (bottom)

piñon, a type of pine tree. The Bannocks fashioned a ball from an animal bladder.

Each of two teams kicked its own ball around a course as many times as set by the leaders. The course led back to the starting place or ran along a track leading to a particular goal, such as trees or a riverbank. Some courses were miles long, and the many **spectators** followed the play on horseback. Among the Cosumnis of California, the individual players, each in his own track, were helped along the course by relays of players waiting at key points. The Mojaves, also of California, used a secondary player who stood behind the single main player and followed him along the track. His only known function seems to have been to give his partner the signal to start.

A good kick could send the ball or stick 30 feet (9 m) into the air and to a distance of 100 feet (30 m) and more. Expert players were so swift they could keep the object in the air almost continuously.

Foot Ball

Foot ball was not as popular among most American Indians as racket and shinny, but it was quite popular with the Inuits. Two teams lined up, facing one another. Barefoot, they tried to kick a ball about the size of a modern softball to a goal. It was considered unacceptable to gain possession of the ball by striking an opponent. The Micmacs, however, would get so engrossed in the game that they were known to scalp an oppo-

Tribes gather on the Montana plains for an opening day parade.

nent to get control of the ball. The practice was eventually stopped. Hair-pulling was used instead.

A variation of foot ball was played on hard snow-covered ground by the Inuits of Labrador and Baffin Island. They used a whip made of sealskin strips to help drive the ball. Men, women, and children played with great determination. The Inuits of western Alaska lined up opposite each other and kicked the ball back and forth between them until it went through the goal. This would score a point and they would start again until they reached a previously agreed-upon score. Games were known to last a day or more.

Some Inuits said that the colored lights in the northern sky were boys playing foot ball. Others believed the lights were ghosts playing with walrus skulls as balls.

Hand-and-Foot Ball

This was one of the few exceptions to the "no-hand" rule in ball games. Hand-and-foot ball was a woman's game in which a large ball was struck down with the hand and kicked back with the foot.

The Inuits of Alaska used two women to play—one to slap the ball and the other to kick it. The Cheyenne used a ball with a thong attached and kept it in play by kicking. Young Cheyenne girls

The Northern Lights

Today we know that the colored lights in the northern sky are caused by electrical discharges from the sun that bounce off the arctic ice. These Northern Lights are also called the aurora borealis.

27

Indian women played jacks or card games together.

counted the number of times they could kick the ball without letting it, or their foot, touch the ground. The Arapahos also held a thong attached to a ball, but they struck it with the hand only (similar to modern-day paddleball without the paddle).

Tossed Ball

Tossed ball was also a hands-on game. The object of the game was to keep a ball constantly in the air. Some tribes, such as the Miamis of Michigan, also strove to keep it out of the hands of an opposing team. The Inuits of Baffin Island played the game during the brief summer, using one man to toss an elaborate fringed ball among the players.

Among the Choctaws, women played a version that resembled today's jacks, tossing the ball in the air as they picked up a small stick from the ground before the ball fell. Zuni boys juggled two balls, made of red clay and the size of chicken eggs, trying to keep one constantly in the air.

Almost a century ago, these Navajo gamblers tried their luck at cards.

Chapter Three

Taking a Chance

Two kinds of games of chance were played by North American Indians, and by most other people around the world: guessing games and dice. Both were played in many variations by men, women, and children, usually in pairs but sometimes in teams. When played as part of a ceremony or ritual, only men competed.

Dice (Also Called Stick Game)

The Passamaquoddy Indians of Maine told this story of dicing:

An old man with great magic powers was able to regain his youth many times by inhaling the breath of young men whom he defeated in dice games. Once again grown old, he searched for a suitable young man to dice with. He found one, but did not know that the young man also possessed magic powers and was protected by the spirit of the air. The old man took up his dice dish, which was formed from a skull, and his dice, which were the eyes of his former victims, and play began. The game was long and exciting, but at each toss made by the young man, the air spirit carried the dice a little higher until they disappeared in the sky. Now the old man, growing ever older, waits to finish the game, and the young man still outwits him.

Indian dice were not the cubes with dots indicating value that we know today. But neither were they eyes, except in legends. They could be the teeth of the beaver or woodchuck, or sticks, split canes, stones, grains of corn, fruit pits, nut shells, or disks made of bone, shells, or pottery. Engraved or painted designs, such as dots, lines, circles, or crosses, were used to

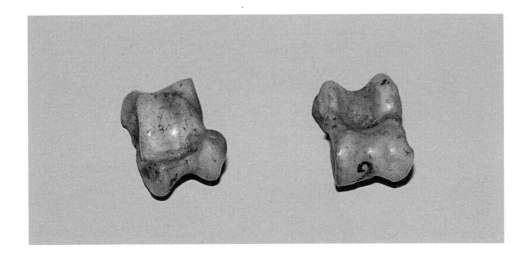

Bone dice, from the Tarahumara tribe

indicate values, which were often not decided upon until game time. The Inuits used dice with **exquisite** little ivory carvings of birds, seals, bears, and people, each of which had an assigned value. Dice and dicing games had many variations.

The dice were either thrown by hand or tossed in a bowl or basket. The winner of a toss was the player who had the most of whatever combinations the players had previously agreed upon. Counters, twigs, or sticks in various sizes or bundles could be passed along by the losers to the winners of each toss, and the winner was the side that finally won all the counters. The dice, sometimes known as slaves or horses, might be moved along a counting board or places marked on the ground by pebbles in a square or circle, advancing as indicated by the dice. If a player's counter fell on an opponent's position, the slave or horse already there was said to be killed and was

Stick dice, made by the Papago

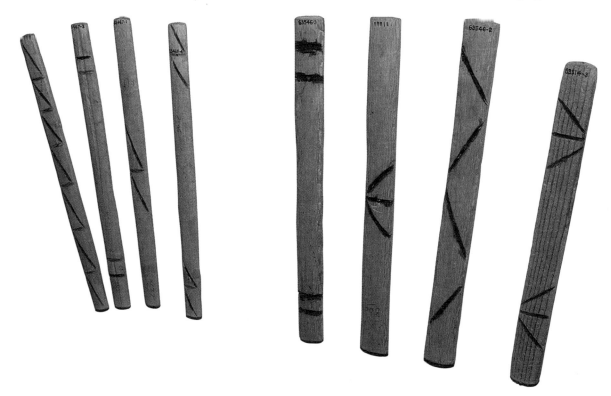

A modern-day shaman performs a ritual.

sent back to its starting place. Other rules about advancing or retreating were made up before the start of the game, and the first player to complete the circuit was the winner. There was no limit to the number of players allowed.

The dice had spiritual meaning beyond that of gambling and chance. The Acomas of New Mexico blew on their dice, as gamesters do today, to ensure good fortune. The Micmacs poured water into their dicing baskets, left them out overnight, and then interpreted the way the water looked in the basket as a sign of either good or evil to come. The shamans of the Delaware and Iroquois threw tobacco onto a fire as they danced the entire night before a large game in a

Shaman

A shaman was believed to be a holy person who could use magic to cure the sick, control events, and foretell the future.

plea to the spirits for a favorable outcome to the game and for the future. Dice games were part of celebrations and of rituals surrounding illness and death. Hoping to please the spirits, the Hurons observed many rituals and **taboos** in the dice games they played to cure illnesses. And four or five days after a death, Dakota men and women played dice for the dead person's property.

Stick Games

Like dice games, stick games were played in every tribe in many ways. Originally the sticks, which could be decorated or left plain, seem to have been broken arrow **shafts.** Later, they were specially made.

The Apache hid a bean in one of these hollow guessing-game sticks.

The sticks were divided into two bundles, and the object of the game was to guess which bundle held an odd number or specially decorated stick. In the East, the sticks were held in the hand. On the Pacific coast, they were hidden in a bundle of shredded bark or, in the Northwest, in a leather container. The games could last for days and were heavily bet on. Among some California tribes, losers would take flints or pieces of glass and cut their legs in crisscrosses from knee to ankle until the blood ran free, hoping to **appease** the spirits who brought them bad luck.

Hand Game (Also Called Button, Button, Who's Got the Button?)

This was the most widespread game among Indians. Versions of the hand game were found in more than eighty tribes. Men, women, and children played, but separately. The hand game was always played indoors, so it was a favorite winter game. One person would hold the "button" while the person seated opposite would guess which hand held the game piece. Sometimes the object was to guess how many pieces were in a hand. At other times, players passed the piece among them while the other side tried to guess where it was. The passers would try to deceive the guessers with gestures and **grimaces.** Meanwhile, the guessers were straining eyes and heads to follow the action.

Score was kept with small sticks, and the team or person with the most or all of the sticks at the end of the game was

Hectic Action

Singing and drum playing accompanied many rounds of the hand game. With men in one area and women in another—each playing and singing to a different drumbeat—the scene could be one of great chaos (and fun).

the winner. If playing for a horse or animal skins or some other particular stake, the number of wins each required was decided upon prior to the game.

Hidden Ball
(Also Called Hidden Moccasin)

The Jicarilla Apaches tell this story of hidden ball:

*When the world was young, it was always dark. The only light came from torches made of the plumes of eagles. The people and animals that went about by day wanted more light, but the night animals—the black bear, the brown bear, the panther, and the owl—wanted to keep things the way they were. They finally agreed to settle the matter by playing a game of hidden ball. In the first game, the sharp-eyed magpie and quail, who loved the light, spotted the stick under which the little gaming piece was hidden and told the people which stick to choose. The morning star came out, and the black bear ran away to hide in the dark underbrush. In the second game, the people were once again guided by the magpie and the quail so that they won. The sky grew brighter in the east, and the brown bear ran away and hid in a dark place. This was repeated a third time, and the sky grew bright, and the panther **sidled** away into the darkness. Then the people played a fourth time and won again with the help of the magpie and quail. And the sun rose over the horizon and lighted the world and it was day, and the owl flew away and hid. And so it was forever more.*

As in the hand game, a ball or other object was hidden and the players had to guess where it was. But in this game, the

Navajos today play hidden ball, using boots instead of moccasins.

hiding place was one of three or four similar objects. The game was also enjoyed by American pioneers.

Indians played with cane tubes or wooden cups. Men sometimes played with moccasins. Although called "hidden ball," the hidden object could be a bean or a stone. Long winter nights were favored for this game. The Navajos played only in darkness because they believed that a player would be struck blind if the sun shone on him as he played. If they were still playing when the sun rose, all the openings to their lodge would be covered with blankets and they would blacken the skin under their eyes.

The hoop dance celebrates the Indian's skill at hoop games.

Chapter Four

Snow-Snakes Don't Bite

Among the Indians of North America, snow-snake, archery, hoop-and-pole, and ring-and-pin were among dozens of games that were primarily tests of individual skill rather than team efforts.

Snow-Snake

North American Indians who lived in snow zones played games in winter with arrows used as darts or **javelins** hurled along ice or into the air to see who could throw farthest. The snow-snake was a

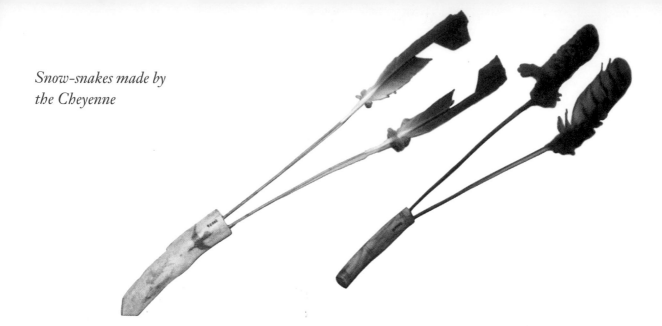

Snow-snakes made by the Cheyenne

Keepsake Snow-Snakes

Among the Pawnees, willow snow-snakes were used as javelins for throwing long distance. When a boy won enough of them, his grandmother wove them into a mat for him.

rod as much as 10 feet (3 m) long and polished to glide more easily along the packed snow or in a rut dug for the purpose. The snakes were often carved and decorated with paints and feathers. The Iroquois sometimes shaped theirs like boats.

Games were played by everyone according to their age and gender. The Crees iced a narrow downhill track for 60 feet (18 m) or more, constructing four snow barriers along the way. The snake, about 8 inches (20 cm) long, was placed at the top and pushed. The snake had to pass through the barriers without leaving the track. Women often played without the barriers along a twisting narrow track.

Archery, Darts, and the Javelin

Games with bows and arrows were for men and boys only. Simply shooting arrows with a bow at a target marked with scores to accumulate points, as is done today, was not considered much of a game to most Indians. Only a few tribes—the

Hopis, the Omahas, and the Montagnais of Labrador—played in this way. However, they usually preferred other bow-and-arrow games. The Omahas shot at arrows embedded in a tree trunk to dislodge them. The Hopis shot or threw arrows so that the feathered ends crossed those of arrows already on the ground. Crossing arrows was also a game among the Inuits, Apaches, Tewas, Zunis, and the Pimas and their relatives, the Tarahumaras of Mexico. The Crow played a two-part game, first shooting at a thin bundle of grass so that it was **impaled** on the arrow, then releasing the bundle into the air and shooting at it again before it hit the ground.

Boys among the Dakotas also shot into the air at bundles of grass. Older boys of the Mandans would try to get as many

Throwing arrows is still a popular sport on the reservation.

arrows into the air at one time as they could. The first arrow they shot had to be very high so that it would stay up long enough for the arrows that followed. Among the Pimas, a boy ran inside a circle of marksmen, dragging a target of rags held by a long cord, hopefully long enough to keep him out of the range of the arrows. Each man then tried to hit the moving target. If he did, he won that round and the stakes, from which he was expected to give the target boy a share.

The Kiowas threw arrows like javelins, aiming to see who could throw farthest. The Chiricahua Apaches used arrows like darts. The first player threw his arrow at a mark on the ground about 10 feet (3 m) away. If he missed, he was out of the game, and his arrow was given to the next player. When the arrow found its mark, the rest of the players took turns shooting their arrows across the one on the ground. Play could go on for some time without anyone accomplishing the feat. But if someone did, all the arrows were his.

Hoop-and-Pole

A hoop and arrow used by the Plains Indians during the 1880s

Played by men, and occasionally boys, throughout North America, hoop-and-pole involved throwing a spear or shooting an arrow through a hoop or ring. It sounds easy, but there were hundreds of rules and methods of scoring that complicated the game.

Often the hoop resembled a spider web and scores depended on which holes the poles went through. In other groups, the hoop was made of an inner and outer ring attached by cords, with no net at all. The small ring of the Pawnees had a single bead inside. Hoops were lashed together with **rawhide** or cord or beads among some tribes, made of corn husks or stone among others. The size of the hoops also varied from under 3 inches (8 cm) among the Paiutes to 25 inches (64 cm) among the Oglala Sioux. The poles were equally diverse. The Apaches used long, jointed poles with rings on the end. The Hopis and Thompsons used poles that are better described as feathered darts.

A champion hoop dancer performs at a tribal event.

The explorers Meriwether Lewis and William Clark, sent by President Thomas Jefferson to explore the Louisiana Territory newly acquired from France, wrote of the Mandans' elegant wooden floor for playing hoop-and-pole. About 40 feet (12 m) long, it ran between two chiefs' lodges. The Creeks played in large, enclosed courts with sloping sides on which spectators were seated. The Apaches played on level ground, cleared for about 100 feet (30 m), with a rock in the center for the player to stand on.

Ring-and-Pin

A miniature version of hoop-and-pole, this game was as popular but was also played by women and children. A ring was attached by a thong to a pin or dart, and the object of play was to toss and then catch the ring on the pin. The "ring" could be bones, pumpkin rinds, or the skull of a small rodent. Notches on the ring indicated points. Game scores could be two or two thousand, but one hundred was usually the winning number.

Foot Races and other Games

Many Indians enjoyed foot races over a variety of distances and **terrains.** Other games included ring toss, throwing stones at a target, sliding stones on ice, cat's cradle, and spinning tops. Tops was the most widely played children's game of winter and was usually played on ice. The Oglala Sioux tried to keep the top spinning by whipping at it. Inuit boys would try to run around their snow or wood igloo before their top stopped spinning. Inuit men would spin a good-natured man around on a top-shaped piece of ice until he got sick!

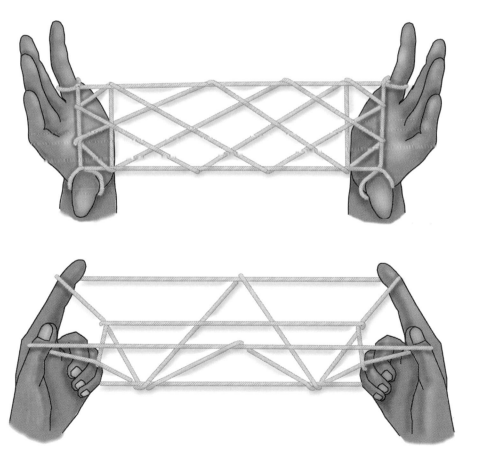

Cat's cradle figures: an Apache Door (top), and Two Mountains and a River (bottom)

Today, Indian games, dances, and rituals are practiced by many tribes at yearly meetings, or powwows.

Chapter Five

Changes in Tribal Life

The role of games in Indian life changed with the opening of Indian lands to white settlement. Many tribes were forced into other areas of the country and onto **reservations**. Tribes grew smaller, and a few disappeared entirely as diseases such as measles and smallpox killed many Indians. Missionaries and federal government officials discouraged the use of games in Indian religious ceremonies. Tribes could not leave reservations to meet one another for competitive games.

49

The Missionary Movement

Missionaries were people sent by a church or religious group to teach the group's faith and to do good works. As part of the missionary movement, missionaries lived among the Indians and taught them Christianity.

Indians had believed that games would appease the spirits into, for example, bringing back the buffalo. But the Indians quickly realized that this was not to be. The once self-sufficient Indians lost the resources and freedom that made games such an important and joyous part of their lives. Fewer players, little money, the realization that games were not going to please the spirits, and the loss of old skills all combined to push games into the background.

The story of the Indian peoples is intertwined with that of the buffalo.

The Indians Adapt to Changes

There were few opportunities on a reservation to earn the money that was fast replacing trade and **barter.** To earn money, many men left to seek work in towns or cities. Many young boys and girls were sent away to government and religious schools to get the education and training needed to get jobs.

Much of tribal life, of which games were such a large part, was lost. Government agencies made inexpensive equipment available, which relieved the Indians of having to make their own balls, rackets, and nets. This made some games easier to play. Non-Indian players and non-Indian games such as cards, checkers, chess, baseball, and basketball became popular.

Indian Games Today

Today, some of the old Indian games, particularly for children, are still played. Navajo children tending flocks of sheep are renowned for their skill at cat's cradle. The Inuit still play snow-snake and many other games they have played for centuries. But today's Indian games are largely American games.

Jim Thorpe

Jim Thorpe was a young boy of Sauk and Fox Indian heritage who was sent to the Indian School at Carlisle, Pennsylvania. He became one of the greatest American athletes of all time.

He was renowned for his football **prowess** and for winning the 1912 Olympics in shot put, hurdles, broad jump, and several foot races. During his amazing career, he played for such teams as the New York Giants, the Cleveland Indians, and the Chicago Cardinals. His Indian name, Wa-Tho-Huk, means "Bright Path."

High school and other team games create much interest and rivalry among the Indians and other Americans of North America.

Choctaw boys playing stickball today.

Glossary

agility—the ability to move fast and easily

anthropologist—a scientist who studies the beliefs and ways of life of different people around the world

appease—to make someone content or calm

barter—to trade by exchanging food or other goods or services, rather than by using money

buckskin—a strong, soft material made from the skin of a deer or sheep

ethnologist—a scientist who studies the racial history of different groups of people

exquisite—highly pleasing due to beauty or perfection

grimace—a tightening and twisting of the face muscles, as in pain or disgust

impaled—pierced with a sharp point

javelin—a light spear that is thrown for distance

plume—a long, fluffy feather often used as an ornament on clothing

propel—to move something forward

prowess—skill or bravery

rawhide—the skin of cattle or other animals before it has been soaked in a special solution and made into leather

reservation—an area of land set aside by the government onto which the American Indians were moved

shaft—the long, narrow rod of an arrow

shuttlecock—a lightweight, cone-shaped object with a rounded tip that is batted by rackets across a net in the game of badminton

sidle—to move away cautiously, in a sideways direction

sinew—a strong fiber or band of tissue that connects a muscle to a bone

spectators—those who watch an event, but do not participate in it

taboo—a rule against touching, doing, or saying something for fear of immediate harm from a supernatural force

terrain—ground, or land

terrapin—a North American turtle that lives in or near fresh water or along seashores

thong—a narrow strip of leather used to fasten things together

To Find Out More

Your school library and local public library will have books on the history of most of the Indian nations mentioned in this book. They may also have information on various tribal celebrations open to the public, including the powwows held in many parts of the country. While you may not see any original native games played, you can see dances, various forms of shelter such as the tepee, and other aspects of native cultures.

Many used bookstores have nineteenth- and early-twentieth-century books and magazines with personal anecdotes of the early days of European contact with the Indians. If you have a museum or historical society near you, these can be interesting sources of information, photographs, and artifacts for you to look at. You can access information on the Internet by name of particular tribes for addresses and phone numbers of tribal councils, or you can write to the Bureau of Indian Affairs, United States Department of the Interior, Washington, D.C. 20245.

Books

Bial, Raymond. *Navajo* (Lifeways series). Tarrytown, NY: Marshall Cavendish, 1998.

Brown, Deni. *Cat's Cradle* (Henderson Activity Packs series). New York: DK Publications, Inc. 1988.

Fleischner, Jennifer. *Inuit: People of the Arctic* (Native Americans series). Brookfield, CT: Millbrook Press, 1995.

Hahn, Elizabeth. *Pawnee* (Native American People series, set III). Vero Beach, FL: Rourke Publications, 1992.

Hoyt-Goldsmith, Diane. *LaCrosse: The National Game of the Iroquois*. New York: Holiday House, 1998.

Long, Barbara. *Jim Thorpe: Legendary Athlete* (Native American Biographies series). Springfield, NJ: Enslow Publications, 1997.

Stein, R. Conrad. *Lewis and Clark* (Cornerstones of Freedom series). Danbury, CT: Children's Press, 1997.

Underwood, Tom. *Cherokee Legends and the Trail of Tears*. Cherokee, NC: Cherokee Publications, 1956.

Organizations and Online Sites

Jim Thorpe
http://www.cmgww.com/sports/thorpe/thorpe.html
The official web site of the legendary Indian athlete, with biography, photos, career highlights, and fascinating facts.

National Indian Athletic Association
4084 Ibex
Salem, OR 97305
This organization promotes and coordinates sports education and activities among the Indian people at local, regional, and national levels.

The Lacrosse Hall of Fame and Museum: Native American History of Lacrosse
http://lacrosse.org/museum/history.htm
This site features a brief history of the game, written by Thomas Vennum, the author of *American Indian Lacrosse: Little Brother of War*.

Toli: The Original Field Sport
http://www.uga.edu/~toli/
This is the home page of the University of Georgia's Toli team, where you can learn all about the history of the Choctaw game.

A Note on Sources

There are hundreds of books with information about games played by the Indians before they were influenced by other cultures. Unfortunately, this information always seems to be contained in a single paragraph or so, and adds up to very little about a lot of regional games (or variations of the same game). One source in particular was definitive. The Report of the Bureau of American Ethnology contains authentic firsthand accounts by Indians and those in early contact with them—missionaries, priests and preachers, army personnel, mountain men, researchers, teachers—which were collected by representatives of the Smithsonian Institution. This report provided the raw material for *North American Indian Games*, which I see as a sculpture. The core was carved and shaped and arranged, as I chipped away here and added there. Bits of information were culled from many other books, and some newspaper and magazine articles, until the sculpture took on the shape most pleasing to me. —*Madelyn Klein Anderson*

Index

Numbers in *italics* indicate illustrations.

About the Author

Madelyn Klein Anderson holds degrees from Hunter College of the City University of New York, New York University, and the Graduate School of Library and Information Science of Pratt Institute in Brooklyn, New York. Before turning to writing full-time, Mrs. Anderson was an army officer, an occupational therapist, an editor of books for young people, and an editorial consultant to the New York City Board of Education. A native New Yorker who has lived in California, Texas, New Mexico, and Alabama, Mrs. Anderson returned to New York and now lives in Manhattan.